Redouté's Finest Flowers in Embroidery

This book is dedicated to the special people in my life
Simon, Stacey and Tessa

First published in 2002 by
Sally Milner Publishing Pty Ltd
PO Box 2104
Bowral NSW 2576
AUSTRALIA
Reprinted 2002
© Trish Burr 2002

Design by Caroline Verity
Editing by Anne Savage
Illustrations and diagrams by Trish Burr and Anna Warren
Photography by Andrew Elton, Tasty Photo & Design

Printed in Hong Kong

National Library of Australia Cataloguing-In-Publication data:

Burr, Trish.
    Redouté's finest flowers in embroidery.

    ISBN 1 86351 293 4.

    1. Redouté, P. J. (Pierre Joseph), 1759-1840. 2.
    Embroidery. 3. Flowers in art. I. Title.

    746.44

Redouté's
Finest Flowers
in Embroidery

TRISH BURR

SALLY MILNER PUBLISHING

Acknowledgements

At the 73rd Annual Academy awards, host Steve Martin offered a television to the recipient who could make the shortest acceptance speech. When Julia Roberts stood up she stated that as she already had a television she had no intention of keeping it short!

Sorry folks—-but I too have a television ...

My thanks go to Sally Milner Publishing who took a chance on an outsider and made it all happen.
To my family for your love and support. To my Fairy Godmother Pat, just an email away, constantly offering support, encouragement, and goodie parcels to keep me going!

To Gill—-you were with me every step of the way, you made me believe in myself and taught me the difference between the Liliaceae and the Iridaceae (I think!).

To Petra, who kept me together and never let me quit.

To those who have helped in their own special way, including: my cheerful friend Janey Millar, Sheila Burr, Sue Burr and Nigel Wilson, Maureen Jooste, Ricky Domnick, Riana Van Der Merwe of Talking Threads magazine and Origin and Future Publishing in the UK.

My thanks go to Patricia Brien and Dollfus Mieg et Cie (DMC) in Paris for the assistance, support and encouragement proffered before and during the writing of this book. Thank you for your permission to use the DMC trademark and for the donation of all the DMC products used throughout this book.

I wish to thank the following for their assistance in research and development: the British Natural History Museum, the British Picture Library Association, TASCHEN, Dan Poynter of Para Publishing and DMC.

This book is dedicated to my husband Simon, who never stopped believing in me and never stopped showing me through his continuous love and support, and to my daughters Stacey and Tessa, whose thoughts and ideas were a constant inspiration and who endlessly cheered me up when I was down in the dumps. We made it happen together.

To my higher power, for the gift that ensures I will have another twelve years of school runs!

Plant illustration, so desirable moreover for the study of botany,

gracefully embellishes the finest products of industry,

sometimes bedecks winter with the finery of spring,

and charms the leisure hours of those whose magical paintbrushes

give lasting existence to the ephemeral gifts of flora.

Pierre Joseph Redouté

Pierre Joseph Redouté (1759—1840) was considered the finest botanical artist of his time. The name of this long dead painter of flowers is usually associated with modern reproductions of his famous paintings of roses, but the subjects of *Les Liliacées* ('The Lily Family'), published in parts in France between 1802 and 1816, and of his last work, *Choix des plus belles fleurs et des plus beaux fruits* ('A Choice of the Most Beautiful Flowers and the Most Beautiful Fruits'), published between 1827 and 1833, rank amongst his most elegant. It is on paintings in these collections that my embroideries have been based. The paintings of the second book depicted a selection of flowers chosen simply for their beauty, and revealed his love of flowers—an expression of life which began in his youth and ended the day before he died, aged 81, when he painted another lily, the source of the final embroidery.

Contents

Acknowledgements 4

Preface 5

Introduction 8

Materials 10

Techniques 14

Tips for working the designs 15

Stitch glossary 16

    Bullion knot 16

    French knot 17

    Long and short stitch 18

    Split stitch 26

    Stem stitch 26

    Seeding stitch 26

    Satin stitch 27

    Padding 28

    Woven picot stitch 29

    Starter sampler 30

The Projects

The Projects...36

Camellia blanc..38

Bengale thé hymenée...41

Sabot des alpes...44

Iris xiphium varieté..47

Convolvulus tricoleur...50

Dahlia double...53

Pavot...56

Magnolia soulangeana..59

Rosa gallica maheka...62

Iris pale...66

Amaryllis brésilienne...70

La dillene..73

Strelitzia..76

Variétés de rose jaune..79

Ipomoea quamoclit...83

Anemone simple..86

Le lys blanc..91

Introduction

Being a self-taught embroiderer, when I began I would often sit for hours, tearing my hair out with frustration, trying to master a stitch with the aid of a diagram. It was such a sense of achievement when I came across a clear illustration with a good explanation, and suddenly it all became clear!

Our doubts are traitors
And make us lose the good we oft might win
By fearing to attempt. Measure for Measure (William Shakespeare)

With this in mind I have compiled this book with diagrams and explanations that aim to guide you through every step of the way.

Just as a good recipe for chocolate chip cookies would be a disaster if one vital ingredient were left out, so also does this apply to an embroidery design. To this end I have included those ingredients in the form of tips.

There is a chapter on materials and equipment with recommendations and alternatives. Residing in a third world country, I have often had difficulty obtaining the correct materials and have become an expert at finding the next best thing. I have also incorporated a stitch glossary, which includes all the stitches needed to complete these designs.

No detail has been spared in an effort to guide you through the embroidery process, and each project is illustrated in both photographic and diagrammatic form to prevent confusion.

The various parts of a plant are stitched separately to differentiate between shapes and shaded areas. For those of you who have never attempted this type of embroidery before or who have worked only cross-stitch or needlepoint, please do not be nervous about having a go.

The wonderful thing about surface embroidery is that it looks much more difficult than it really is—you could even say it is a bit like painting by numbers, with the added advantage of no counting! Begin with the starter sampler and you will be amazed to find that you have unleashed a creative side that you never knew you had.

The more experienced stitcher will relish the prospect of working on something as beautiful and enduring as the artwork of Pierre Joseph Redouté. We learn something new every day, so hopefully this book, with its new approach, will benefit you in some small way.

I have enjoyed compiling these designs for you and it is my greatest wish that you in turn will derive similar pleasure.

Uses for your embroidery—another wonderful thing about embroidery is its versatility. The

designs can be embroidered on any suitable fabric item, such as articles of clothing, sheets, pillowcases, cushion covers, duvets, bathroom sets, towels, linen and laundry bags, nightwear, spectacle cases or tote bags.

If you are not a sewer, then it is a good idea to purchase ready-made items suitable for embroidering on. Otherwise, get your sewing machine out and make up your finished embroidery into an item of your choice.

Alternatively, you can take the finished embroidery to a good framer, who will stretch it, mount it and frame it. The pictures can be grouped or done individually, the choice is yours.

Materials

FABRIC

Any type of medium weight cotton or linen fabric can be used for this type of embroidery, as long as it does not stretch. The general requirement is that it should be closely woven and of medium weight.

Any kind of embroidery taking up a large proportion of the fabric needs to be kept taut in a hoop or frame. If the fabric is stretched while the embroidery is in progress it will contract and become distorted when removed from the hoop.

Suitable cotton fabrics include:
• *Calico*
• *Any type of medium weight closely woven cotton*
• *Polyester cotton*
• *Cotton satin*

Suitable linen fabrics include:
• *Kingston 55 count*
• *Church linen*
• *Any type of medium weight closely woven linen*
• *Dowlas*

BACKING FABRIC

Backing fabric is essential for this type of embroidery. It is used behind the embroidery fabric and helps prevent distortion. I have worked embroideries with and without backing fabric and the results are much better with. The general rule is that it should be lightweight. Take the backing fabric and place behind the top fabric. Iron both pieces flat together and mount into a hoop. Check that there are no creases in the backing fabric and stretch accordingly until both top and back fabrics are flat and evenly mounted.
If you prefer you can tack the backing and top fabric together before mounting, but this is not necessary.

Suitable backing fabrics include:
• *Muslin (first choice)*
• *Lightweight cotton*
• *Lightweight calico*

THREADS

I have used DMC Mouliné special 6 strand cotton, which is available in 464 colours. (At the time of going to press I understand that an additional 27 colours have been released.) DMC six strand embroidery floss is the most widely sold embroidery thread in the world and to my mind is the best quality. It is composed of six easily separated strands, so that you can use one or more strands of the same colour, or mix colours to obtain a shaded effect. It is made from the finest long staple cottons, and is the result of years of experience. Double mercerisation gives the cottons a high sheen and they are absolutely colourfast and fade-resistant, ensuring your work can be passed from generation to generation.

Last year I had the good fortune to visit the factory in Mulhouse, France, where we saw the thread production. It is a humbling experience to see the intensive process involved in producing the finished skein of thread. To reproduce consistent dye lots strict adherence to previous dye solutions is monitored under the carefully critical eye of colour checkers who have spent many years perfecting the art and are employed solely for this task.

Despite this, it remains important to purchase enough thread from the same dye lot to complete the one embroidery, as dye lots unavoidably differ, even if only to the slightest degree.

The other thread that I have used for the finer details is DMC machine embroidery thread.

OTHER THREADS

Other threads manufactured by DMC include:
- *Metallic threads*
- *Rayon with a high sheen*
- *Medicis crewel wool*

As long as the strands are divisible or the thread is fine enough, any of these can be used in conjunction with DMC cottons to add texture and interest to your embroidery.

TIPS

- *Pull out the number of strands you wish to use in the one action, not as single strands.*
- *Keep your thread length at a maximum of about 20 inches (50 cm), to prevent tangling and knotting.*
- *Dangle your needle and thread from the back of your work at intervals to undo twists and prevent tangling.*

TIPS

- *When you have tightened the fabric in the hoop as much as possible, hold it over the steam from a kettle or a saucepan of boiling water until just damp. Allow to dry and the fabric will become drum tight.*

HOOPS

An embroidery hoop is essential for this style of embroidery. It is imperative that the fabric be kept taut as you work, as otherwise it cannot support the weight of the padding and stitching. One of my favourite styles of hoop is the plastic flexi-hoop. It is easy to get the fabric into, and unlike the wooden hoop does not have an opening for the screw, which can often leave a weakness in one area of the fabric. The plastic hoop is light and leaves no marks on the fabric, as can happen with a wooden hoop. Try one and see how you feel; it is a totally personal thing as to which hoop or frame you feel comfortable with. Use the smallest hoop that you can, without encroaching too much on your design. The border between the design and the hoop edge should be a minimum of 3/4 inch (2 cm).

Recommended hoops
- *Plastic flexi-hoop*
- *Wooden embroidery ring with screw for tightening*
- *Wooden frame*

Binding
To avoid the risk of the hoop leaving a dirty ring on your work, I recommend that you bind all hoops before putting the embroidery fabric in place. To do this take bias binding (opened out flat), or a narrow strip of waste cotton fabric, and bind it around the hoop, catching the end with a couple of stitches to prevent slipping.

Preventing fraying
There are numerous methods of preventing the edges of your embroidery fabric from fraying, but binding them with masking tape is by far the easiest. You might prefer to use Fraystop liquid, or to overcast the edges on the sewing machine

SCISSORS

You will need a small, sharp pair of embroidery scissors for cutting threads. It is worth spending a little extra and getting the best pair that you can afford. Be brutal in your resolution to keep your embroidery scissors for cutting threads only—not fabric, paper or anything else. This is a constant bone of contention in my house, for I far too often find my precious scissors blunt and covered with glue, having been misappropriated for use on thick cardboard homework projects!

NEEDLES

There are quite a number of different needles suitable for various needlecraft projects. The choice can be confusing so I will keep it to the basics needed for the embroidery designs in this book. Again, always buy the best quality needles you can afford. As soon as the needle you are using becomes blackened or does not slip easily through the fabric, change it for a new one.

Recommended needles

Embroidery needles (for most embroidery stitches):
* *size 10 for one strand of thread*
* *size 9 for two strands of thread*
* *size 8 for three or more strands*

Straw or milliner's needles (for French knots or bullion knots):
* *size 4 for one/two strands of thread*
* *size 3 for two/three strands of thread*

My favourite brands are Milwards and DMC, but your personal preference may be for other brands.

Techniques

Outlines for transferring each design are supplied in this book, but can be reduced or enlarged according to your personal preference. The easiest way to do this is by photocopying. Do remember that if you reduce a design in size, the number of embroidery stitches will also be reduced, and could limit the shading that can be applied, just as enlarging a design will increase the number of stitches needed to fill the outlines. You cannot reduce or enlarge the actual stitch sizes, as this will give a very uneven finish.

There are a number of ways to transfer a design onto fabric, but by far the easiest is to place the piece of fabric on top of the design, with a light source behind the design, and trace over it with a soft HB pencil onto the fabric.

Tracing methods
- *Use a light box*
- *Place a light under a glass table*
- *Hold fabric and design up against a glass window (you will need to attach both with masking tape to prevent movement)*

Another method uses fabric carbon paper; in this case you place the carbon between the design and the fabric (design on top, fabric underneath) and draw over the design with a sharp pencil.

Directional lines

It is helpful to draw directional lines onto the fabric after transferring the design. Using a sharp pencil, draw in a few lines to remind you in which direction the stitches travel

TIPS FOR WORKING THE DESIGNS

- Trace the outline onto the fabric, following the transfer instructions.
- Fill in details and direction lines with a pencil, following the padding and details illustrations for the project you are working.
- Tack the backing fabric in place.
- Mount the fabric into the hoop, following the instructions.
- Use the colour chart as a guide to thread colours, and the colour photo for details on shading. Note, however, that I have distorted the colours on the colour charts to make it easier to see where one colour ends and another begins. The photograph of the finished embroidery is the ultimate guide.
- Follow the step-by-step directions on the instruction page.
- Always work from the background towards the foreground.
- Outline all shapes with split stitch to give them a neat raised edge.
- Work stems in split stitch.
- Work padded areas with padding or satin stitch.
- Leave a gap between pieces of padding to create a three-dimensional illusion.
- When using long and short stitch, always work from the outside in unless the directions say otherwise.
- Where possible, shade from light to dark.
- Avoid abrupt changes of colour in your shading.
- Work centre leaf veins in split stitch in the lightest shade used in the leaf, unless the directions say otherwise.
- If you are uncertain about the way a flower is constructed, study a living flower if possible, and work accordingly.
- Stems always come from the midpoint of the leaf end, and from the centre of the flower.
- Do not try to put in every little plant detail in the first layer of stitchery; rather, work these in afterwards.
- A flower has a centre; the petals have to be attached to this centre, which contain stamens or lumps of pollen. The petals should be worked towards this centre and any stamens or pollen added afterwards. If this is not always obvious, take apart a real flower to understand better how it works.

Stitch Glossary

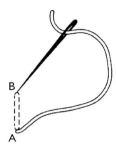

Step 1

Using 2 strands of thread and needle size 10 bring the needle up at A and down at B.

Step 2

Bring the needle partly up at A, leaving a long loop.

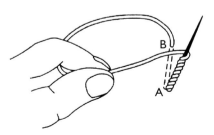

Step 3

Hold the loop between thumb and forefinger and wind thread around the needle anti-clockwise. The number of loops depends upon the length of the bullion required. Ten loops will give you a long bullion, 20 loops a very long one.

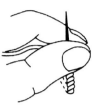

Step 4

Hold the needle and coil with the thumb and forefinger of one hand and pull the needle gently through the coil with the other hand.

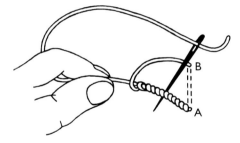

Step 5

Push the top of the coil down while pulling the thread through. Even out the coil by pushing it along the thread until it lies flat on the fabric.

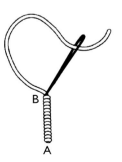

Step 6

Re-insert the needle at B and take the thread through ready to start the next stitch.

FRENCH KNOT

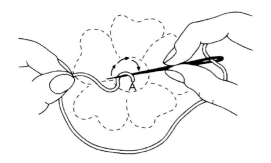

Step 1
Using 2 strands of thread and straw needle size 4, bring the thread up at A. Hold the thread between thumb and forefinger as illustrated. Loop the thread over the needle twice. The number of loops depends on how big you require the knot to be, but 2 loops are average.

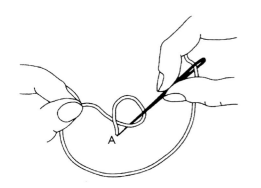

Step 2
Insert the needle into the fabric at A, close to the original hole but not in the same hole.

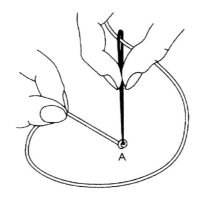

Step 3
Pull the loop taut to form the knot.

LONG AND SHORT STITCH

Long and short stitch is also referred to as silk shading, long and short shading or needlepainting, as the varying stitch lengths encroaching on each other lend this technique wonderfully to shading and give a realistic 'painted' finish.

Long and short stitch is used as a filling stitch for all types of larger shapes, and is the most widely used stitch in this book and therefore worth spending time practicing.

There are a few ground rules for long and short stitch that we will explore in the techniques which follow; once you have mastered these we can look at ideas for enhancing the stitch by various means.

Basic long and short stitch in one direction

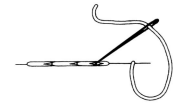

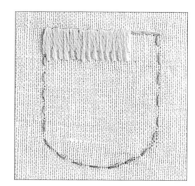

Step 1
Outline the edges of the shape with split stitch. Use 1 strand of the lightest shade of thread required for that element of the design to work the outline. (I have used a darker thread in the photograph for the purpose of demonstration.)
The split stitch forms the foundation for the long and short stitch infill.

Step 2

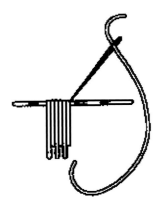

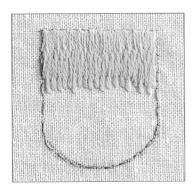

Work the first row in long and short stitch, using the lightest shade of thread. Bring the needle up through the fabric inside the shape, and down over the split stitch line, as this will ensure a neat even edge. Do not make your stitches too small, as this will give an uneven finish. The long stitches should be approximately 5/16 inch (8 mm) in length and the short stitches about three-quarters of that length. Work the 2nd row in long stitch only, using the next darkest shade of thread. In this row bring the needle up through the fabric to split the ends of the previous stitches, and down into the fabric. Although these stitches are worked in

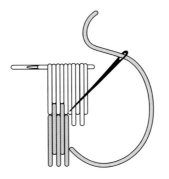

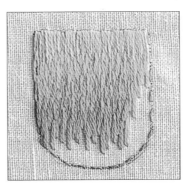

long stitch only, vary their lengths slightly to give a soft uneven line, not a straight one. Long and short stitch is intended to produce soft blending tones so avoid abrupt changes of tone.

Step 3

Work the 3rd and subsequent rows as for the 2nd row. Continue to change the shades of thread to create a shaded look.

DIRECTIONAL LONG AND SHORT STITCH

Shading does not always follow a straight course but can take different directions. If you study the structure of a petal, for example, you will see that it most often tapers towards the centre.

It is a good idea to study some of the plants in your garden to gain a perspective of how they grow; this will be immensely helpful when working out the direction of your stitches.

Filling a shape such as a petal

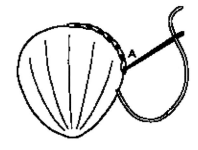

Step 1
Outline the shape with split stitch. This split stitch will form the foundation for the shape to be worked. Pencil in the guidelines.

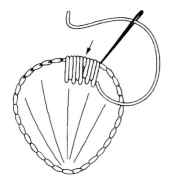

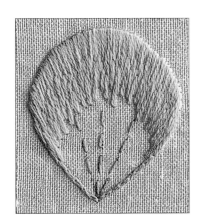

Step 2

Work the first row in long and short stitch, using the lightest shade of thread. Start from the centre tip of the petal and work towards one side. Bring the needle up through the fabric and down over the split stitch line to form a neat edge. Add an extra small stitch occasionally to adjust for the tapering shape. This stitch will subtly alter the direction of subsequent stitches. Remember to keep your stitches a good length. If they become too small the work will not look smooth. Complete the row by working from the centre tip towards the other side.

Work the 2nd row in long stitch only, using the next

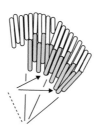

darkest shade of thread. Again work from the centre outward, to one side and then the other. In this row bring the needle up through the fabric, splitting into the base of the previous stitches, and back down below. Vary the length of these stitches slightly to give a soft look to the shading. Work two long stitches into the same point at intervals to adjust for the narrowing space.

Step 3

Work the 3rd row as for the 2nd, using the next darkest shade of thread. Again work from the centre outward, to one side and then the other. Split back into the previous merged stitches as though they were one stitch.

SLANTING LONG AND SHORT STITCH

Filling a smooth-edged leaf

Outline the leaf shape and centre vein with split stitch, using the lightest colour thread. Draw in the guidelines with a pencil.

Starting from the outside right edge, and using the lightest colour, work adjoining long and short stitches towards the centre vein. Follow the angle of the guidelines. Continue working the 2nd and 3rd rows in long stitch only, using the next two darkest shades of thread, until you reach the centre vein.

Starting from the outside left edge and using the darkest colour, work adjoining long and short stitches towards the centre vein. Follow the angle of the guidelines. Continue working the 2nd and subsequent rows in long stitch only, using the next lightest shades of thread, until you reach the centre vein.

Having the contrasting light and dark colours meeting at the central vein gives depth to the leaf. Lastly, take one strand of the lightest shade of thread and work the centre vein in split stitch.

Filling an irregular shape

Although long and short stitch is generally worked from the outside edge in towards the centre, with an irregular shape like this it is best to work from the centre outwards. Outline the shape with split stitch. Pencil in the guidelines. Work the long and short stitch from the centre split stitch line out towards the edge, following the guidelines. Work the long and short stitch from the centre vein line out towards the edge, following the guidelines. Lastly, take one strand of the lightest shade of thread and work over the centre vein in split stitch.

BEYOND THE BASICS:
ENHANCING LONG AND SHORT STITCH

Once you have mastered the basics of long and short stitch and are confident with the shading techniques, you can begin to expand on these techniques. Below are a few tips for adding a more realistic finish to your work.

Areas highlighted in lighter colour Work over stitching with 1 strand of a lighter colour.

Areas shaded in darker colour to add depth Work over stitching with 1 strand of a darker colour.

Outline areas in split stitch in 1 strand of lightest shade to give definition, for example, to the lacy edge of a petal.

Use 2 strands of thread in the needle, in two different colours, to give a streaky effect.

To create texture, use different types of thread in the one piece of work, for example, crewel wool and stranded cotton. Use 1 strand of DMC machine embroidery thread to work very fine details.

SPLIT STITCH

Split stitch is a variation of a simple backstitch, used to outline shapes and sometimes to work details such as stems.

Commencing with a backstitch, split each preceding stitch with the needle to form the next backstitch.

STEM STITCH

Stem stitch is used to work lines such as stems.

The stitches are worked from left to right and overlap each other, without splitting, to form a fine line.

SEEDING STITCH

This stitch is used to indicate tiny little seeds, usually in a flower centre.

Work short straight stitches in different directions, directly onto the fabric. They are normally worked over other embroidery stitches.

SATIN STITCH

Satin stitch is used as a filling stitch where a shape is too small to use long and short stitch.

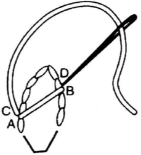
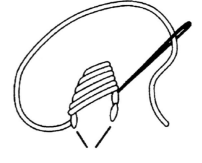

Step 1
Outline the shape with split stitch.

Step 2
Start from the middle of the shape and work out towards the tip, angling the stitches on the diagonal—up at A, down at B, up at C, down at D.

Step 3
Return from the tip to the middle of the shape, slipping the thread under the stitches at the back of the work, and fill the lower half.

PADDING

Padding is used to raise certain areas to create depth. There are two methods. For larger areas you use actual padding material under long and short stitch. For small areas you use two layers of satin stitch.

Long and short stitch over padding

Outline the area to be padded in split stitch. Cut padding material to fit just within each area as shown in the diagram, leaving approximately 1 mm clearance, and slip stitch into place.

You can cut the padded shapes freehand, then trim them to fit, or you can trace the shape onto the padding material with a fine felt-tip pen and cut around it.

When all the padded shapes are in position, embroider over the top with long and short stitch as usual.

Padding with satin stitch

Occasionally an area will be too small to fit in a piece of padding material; in this case you can raise the area with satin stitch.

Step 1

Outline the shape with split stitch.

Step 2

Fill the area with satin stitch on the diagonal, running in the opposite direction to the final layer, taking the needle up and down just inside the split stitch outline.

Step 3

Work over the shape with a 2nd layer of satin stitch, working on the opposite diagonal, and taking the needle up and down just outside the split stitch outline.

WOVEN PICOT STITCH

This stitch is used to create areas of stitching that stand away from the fabric and create a three-dimensional effect.
It is generally used for very small leaves or for the leaves of the calyx at the base of a flower.

Step 1

Insert a pin into the fabric at the point where you want the picot to start.

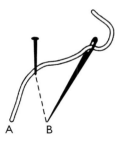

Step 2

Use two strands of thread. Bring the needle up at A, around the pin and down at B.

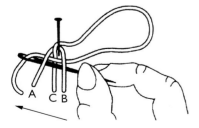

Step 3

Bring the needle up at C, then turn it around in your fingers to use the eye for weaving. Weave the thread in and out as shown, starting next to the pin.

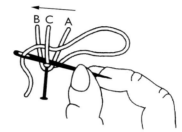

Step 4

Turn your work around and weave a second row. Turn again and weave back, pushing the weaving back towards the pin from time to time.

Step 5

When you have filled the picot to the points A, B, C, the weaving is complete. Make a small backstitch to finish off and remove the pin.
The picot will fall away from the fabric at the tip.

STARTER PROJECT

This project is designed to enable you to practice all the stitches needed to complete any one of the following projects.

Detailed instructions appear on the following pages.

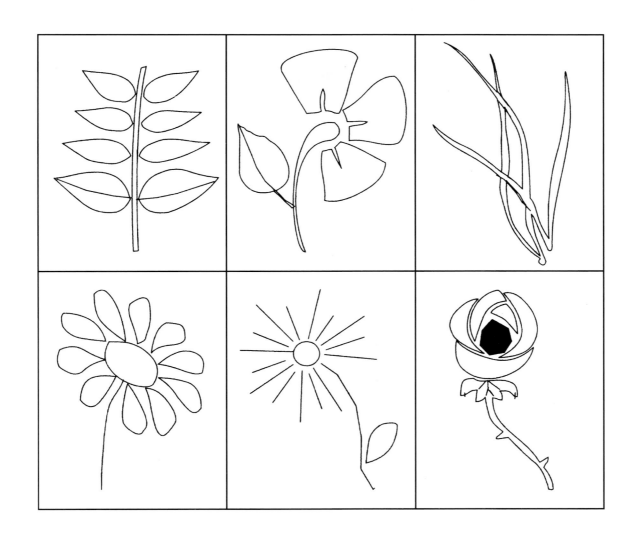

Key	Colour	DMCno	Key	Colour	DMCno
1	Light green	3348	5	Blue	312
2	Green	3347	6	Light yellow	744
3	Dark green	3345	7	Yellow	743
4	Light blue	3755	8	Dark yellow	742

Note: the colours used in the colour key are not accurately matched to DMC thread colours, and are intended as a shading guide only.

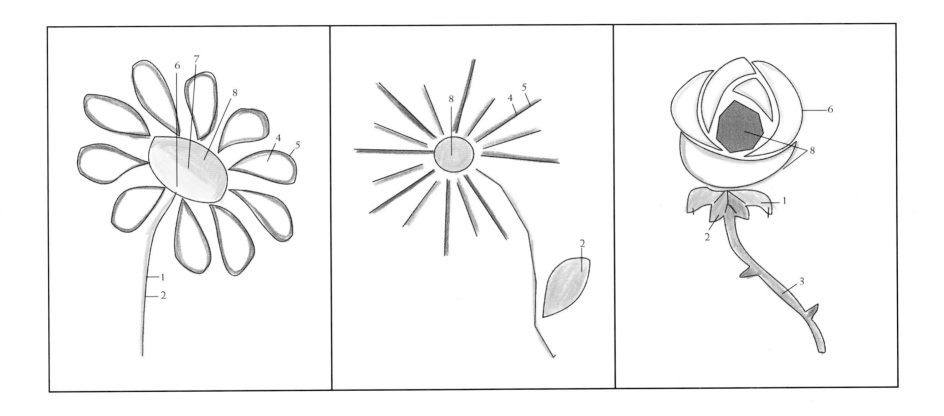

Key	Colour	DMCno		Key	Colour	DMCno
1	Light green	3348		5	Blue	312
2	Green	3347		6	Light yellow	744
3	Dark green	3345		7	Yellow	743
4	Light blue	3755		8	Dark yellow	742

Note: the colours used in the colour key are not accurately matched to DMC thread colours, and are intended as a shading guide only.

Refer back to the stitch glossary for details.

Leaves—Satin stitch

Work main stem in stem stitch using 1 strand of dark green thread. Outline leaves in split stitch using 1 strand of green. Pad all leaves with satin stitch using 1 strand of green. Fill leaves (on top of padding) in satin stitch, using 1 strand of the various shades of green as indicated on the colour chart. On the bottom leaves work away from the centre vein, working the satin stitch at an angle towards the outer edge of leaf. Work the centre veins of the two lowest leaves in split stitch using 1 strand of light green.

Yellow flower—long and short stitch

Work the fine part of the stem in stem stitch, using 1 strand of green, and continue in stem stitch to outline the upper part. Fill the upper part of stem in satin stitch, using 1 strand of lightest green. Outline the leaf in split stitch, using 1 strand of dark green. Fill leaf in long and short stitch, working from the centre vein towards the outer edge. Shade leaf in each shade of green. Work centre vein in split stitch using 1 strand of light green. Outline petals in split stitch using 1 strand of yellow. Fill petals in long and short stitch, using 1 strand at a time of each shade of yellow. Work from outer edges towards the centre, shading from light to dark.

Grasses—Stem stitch

Work grasses in adjoining rows of stem stitch, starting with dark green and shading towards light green. Work approximately three rows, being guided by the photograph of the finished embroidery.

Blue daisy flower—French knots

Work stem in stem stitch using 1 strand of light green. Work over padding in satin stitch in 1 strand of dark green. Outline petals in split stitch using 2 strands of blue. Work flower centre in French knots, using 2 strands of either light yellow or dark yellow, and placing knots to shade from base to top.

Blue ray flower—Bullion knots

Work stem in stem stitch using 1 strand of green. Outline leaf in split stitch using 1 strand of green. Pad leaf in satin stitch, using 1 strand of green. Work over padding in satin stitch using 1 strand of green. Work flower centre in French knots using 2 strands of dark yellow. Work straight petals in bullion knots, using approximately 10 wraps for the shorter petals and 15 for the longer ones—you will have to judge the lengths accordingly. Use 2 strands of light blue on one petal and 2 strands of blue on the next, alternating colours as shown.

Rose—Woven picots

Work stem in stem stitch using 2 strands of dark green. Work small straight stitches for thorns in the same colour. Outline each section of flower in split stitch using 2 strands of yellow. Fill rose centre with satin stitch, using 1 strand of dark yellow. Work 4 woven picots at base of rose, using 1 strand of light green plus 1 strand of green together for the two outer picots, and 1 strand of green with 1 strand of dark green together for the inner picots. Bend the woven picot into a position that resembles a realistic rose sepal. When you are happy with the effect, place a small stitch at the side to hold in place.

You have now practiced all the stitches necessary to complete the projects in this book!

Camellia blanc   Bengale thé hymenée   Sabot des alpes
Dahlia double   Pavot   Magnolia soulangeana   Rosa g
La dillene   Strelitzia   Variétés de rose jaune   Ipomoea

The Projects

Iris xiphium varieté   Convolvulus tricoleur
ica maheka Iris pale Amaryllis brésilienne
uamoclit Anemone simple Le lys blanc

(plate 52 from Choix des plus belles fleurs et des plus beaux fruits)

Materials

- fabric in ecru, 10 x 10 inches (25 x 25 cm)
- DMC stranded cottons in colours listed in key
- needles
  embroidery size 10, for single strand
  embroidery size 9, for 2 strands
  straw size 4, for French knots
- padding

Key	Colour	DMC no	Key	Colour	DMC no
1	White	blanc	8	Very dark green	3051
2	Off white	ecru	9	Dark yellow	783
3	Beige	644	10	Pale yellow	3078
4	Dark beige	642	11	Light gold	3046
5	Light green	369	12	Gold	834
6	Green	3053	13	Dark gold	831
7	Dark green	3052			

▪ Padded areas

▨ Padded areas using satin stitch

▱ Directional and detail lines

Note: the colours used in the colour key are not accurately matched to DMC thread colours, and are intended as a shading guide only.

Stem

Work stem in adjoining rows of stem stitch using 1 strand of each shade of green.

Leaves

Outline leaves in split stitch using 1 strand of dark green. Pad leaves as shown. Fill leaves in long and short stitch using 1 strand of each shade of green. Work from outer edges towards centre vein, shading from light to dark and dark to light as indicated. Work centre veins in split stitch using 1 strand of light green.

Bud

Outline bud in split stitch using 1 strand of dark yellow. Pad each section in satin stitch with 1 strand of yellow. Fill in each section with satin stitch using colours as indicated on chart. Work outlines again in split stitch using 1 strand dark yellow

Petals

Outline petals in split stitch using 1 strand of light yellow. Pad petals as shown. Fill petals with long and short stitch using 1 strand of each shade from white through to dark beige as indicated on chart. Work from outer edge towards centre using directional lines as a guide.

Centre

Fill centre of flower with long straight stitches using 2 strands of yellow. Fill outer part of centre with long straight stitches using 2 strands of yellow. Work French knots around centre using 2 strands of thread (1 strand each of light gold and dark gold in needle).

(from Les Liliacées)

Materials

- fabric in ecru, 10 x 10 inches (25 x 25 cm)
- DMC stranded cottons in colours listed in key
- needles
    embroidery size 10, for single strand
    embroidery size 9, for 2 strands
    straw size 4, for French knots
- padding

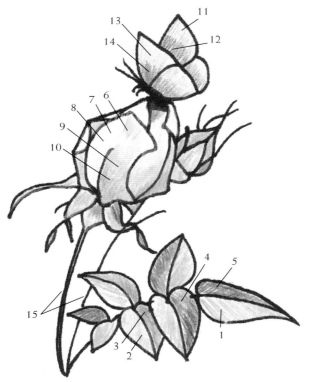

Key	Colour	DMC no	Key	Colour	DMC no
1	Pale green	472	9	Pink	224
2	Light green	471	10	Dark pink	223
3	Green	470	11	Light blue	3839
4	Dark green	469	12	Dark blue	792
5	Very dark green	936	13	Beige	738
6	Light yellow	745	14	Dark beige	437
7	Pale pink	3770	15	Dark green machine embroidery thread	
8	Light pink	225			

Padded areas

Padded areas using satin stitch

Directional and detail lines

Note: the colours used in the colour key are not accurately matched to DMC thread colours, and are intended as a shading guide only.

Stems

Work stems in adjoining rows of stem stitch using 1 strand of very dark green, light green and pale green.

Leaves

Outline leaves in split stitch in 1 strand dark green. Pad leaves as shown. Fill leaves with long and short stitch using 1 strand of each shade of green. Shade from light to dark and dark to light, working from outer edges towards centre vein. Work veins and thorns in split stitch using 1 strand of dark green machine embroidery thread.

Sepals

Outline sepals and calyces for both flower and bud in split stitch, using 1 strand dark green. Pad calyx areas as shown with satin stitch. Fill calyces and sepals with long and short stitch, using 1 strand of each shade of green. Work delicate tips of sepals with split stitch in 1 strand light green.

Rosebud

Outline bud in split stitch using 1 strand dark

pink. Fill bud with long and short stitch using 1 strand of dark pink and light yellow.

Rose

Outline petals with split stitch using 1 strand dark pink. Pad closest petal as shown. Fill petals in long and short stitch, or satin stitch, following the photograph, using 1 strand of each shade of pink. Follow colour chart for directional lines. Outline petals with split stitch for definition, using 1 strand of pale pink.

Butterfly

Outline wings with split stitch using 1 strand dark blue. Pad areas as shown.
Fill back wings in long and short stitch using 1 strand of each shade of blue. Fill front wings in long and short stitch using 1 strand of each shade of beige.
Using 1 strand of dark brown machine embroidery thread, outline body, wings and feelers in split stitch, fill body in satin stitch and work French knots for eyes, tips of antennae, and spots on wings.

(plate 33 from Choix des plus belles fleurs et des plus beaux fruits)

Materials

- fabric in ecru, 10 x 10 inches (25 x 25 cm)
- DMC stranded cottons in colours listed in key
- needles
    embroidery size 10, for single strand
    embroidery size 9, for 2 strands
    straw size 4, for French knots
- padding

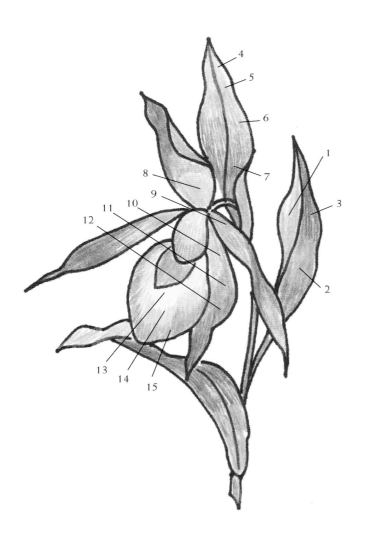

Key	Colour	DMC no
1	Light leaf green	472
2	Leaf green	470
3	Dark leaf green	469
4	Light green	523
5	Green	3364
6	Dark green	3363
7	Very dark green	3362
8	Light orange	3827
9	Orange	977
19	Light brown	434
11	Brown	801
12	Dark brown	838
13	Light yellow	3822
14	Dark yellow	3852
15	Very dark yellow	680

Note: the colours used in the colour key are not accurately matched to DMC thread colours, and are intended as a shading guide only.

Stems

Work stems in adjoining lines of stem stitch using 1 strand of each shade of green.

Leaves

Outline leaves in split stitch in 1 strand of dark green. Pad areas as shown. Fill leaves in long and short stitch using 1 strand of each shade of green. Shade from light to dark. Work overlaps of leaf edges in split stitch using 1 strand of light green.

Petals

Outline petals in split stitch using 1 strand of brown. Fill petals in long and short stitch, using 1 strand of shades of orange and brown, shading from light to dark. Enhance edges with split stitch using 1 strand of light yellow.

Flower body

Outline body in split stitch using 1 strand dark yellow. Pad as shown. Fill body in long and short stitch using 1 strand in each shade of yellow. Shade from light to dark from inside to outside. Work over shadow in 1 strand of very dark yellow.

Centre body

Outline body in split stitch using 1 strand dark yellow. Double pad this area (small piece first and large piece on top). Fill body in long and short stitch using 1 strand of each shade of yellow.

▨	*Padded areas*
▨	*Padded areas using satin stitch*
▱	*Directional and detail lines*

IRIS XIPHIUM VARIETÉ

(plate 30 from Choix des plus belles fleurs et des plus beaux fruits)

Materials

- fabric in ecru, 10 x 10 inches (25 x 25 cm)
- DMC stranded cottons in colours listed in key
- needles
    embroidery size 10, for single strand
    embroidery size 9, for 2 strands
    straw size 4, for French knots
- padding

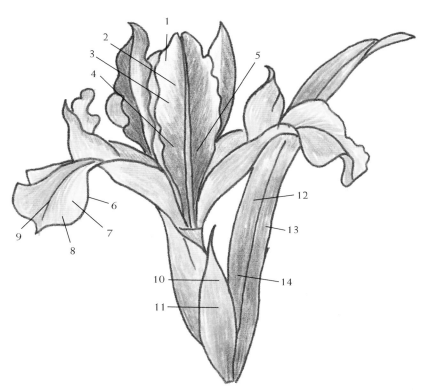

Key	Colour	DMC no	Key	Colour	DMC no
1	Pale blue	3841	8	Dark yellow	783
2	Light blue	3840	9	Rust	976
3	Blue	3839	10	Pale green	734
4	Dark blue	3838	11	Light green	733
5	Very dark blue	792	12	Green	470
6	Light yellow	727	13	Dark green	904
7	Yellow	3821	14	Very dark green	935

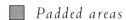

�	Padded areas
▨	Padded areas using satin stitch
◪	Directional and detail lines

Note: the colours used in the colour key are not accurately matched to DMC thread colours, and are intended as a shading guide only.

Leaf

Outline leaf in split stitch using 1 strand dark green. Fill leaf in long and short stitch using 1 strand of each shade of green. Work centre vein in split stitch using 1 strand of very dark green.

Blue petals

Outline petals in split stitch using 1 strand blue. Pad petals as shown. Fill petals in long and short stitch using 1 strand of each shade of blue. Work centre veins in adjoining rows of split stitch using 1 strand of each shade of yellow.

Yellow petals

Outline petals in split stitch using 1 strand yellow. Pad petals as shown. Fill upper surfaces of petals in long and short stitch using 1 strand of each shade of yellow, and blue where appropriate. Fill undersides of petals in long and short stitch using 1 strand in shades of yellow and green.

Bud leaves

Outline leaves in split stitch using 1 strand of dark green. Pad areas as shown. Fill leaves in long and short stitch using 1 strand of each shade from yellow to very dark green. Outline right side and centre vein of front leaf with split stitch in 1 strand of dark green.

CONVOLVULUS TRICOLEUR

(plate 110 from Choix des plus belles fleurs et des plus beaux fruits)

Materials

- fabric in ecru, 10 x 10 inches (25 x 25 cm)
- DMC stranded cottons in colours listed in key
- needles
    embroidery size 10, for single strand
    embroidery size 9, for 2 strands
    straw size 4, for French knots
- padding

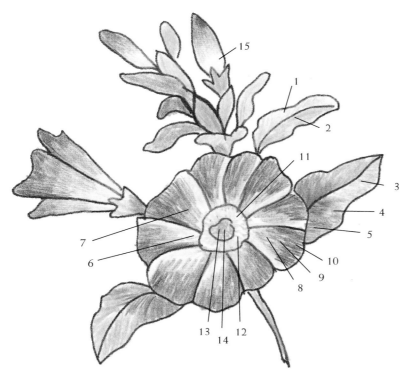

Key	Colour	DMCno	Key	Colour	DMCno
1	Pale green	3348	9	Dark blue	312
2	Light green	989	10	Very dark blue	311
3	Green	988	11	Pale yellow	727
4	Dark green	987	12	Yellow	725
5	Very dark green	895	13	Dark yellow	3820
6	Pale blue	3841	14	Gold	732
7	Light blue	3755	15	White	blanc
8	Blue	334			

■ Padded areas

▨ Padded areas using satin stitch

◩ Directional and detail lines

Note: the colours used in the colour key are not accurately matched to DMC thread colours, and are intended as a shading guide only.

Stem and leaves

Work stem in adjoining rows of stem stitch using 1 strand of each shade of green. Outline leaves in split stitch using 1 strand of dark green. Pad leaves as shown. Fill small leaves in satin stitch, and the larger leaves in long and short stitch, using 1 strand of each shade of green. Work centre veins in split stitch using 1 strand of dark green machine embroidery thread. Outline parts of the small leaves and bud calyces in split stitch using 1 strand of dark green machine embroidery thread.

Buds

Outline buds in split stitch using 1 strand of blue. Pad areas in satin stitch as shown. Fill buds in long and short stitch using 1 strand of each shade of blue, and a little pale yellow at base. Work from outer edges towards centre, shading from dark to light.

Flower

Outline petals in split stitch using 1 strand dark blue. Pad petals as shown. Fill petals with long and short stitch using 1 strand of each shade of blue. Work from outer edge towards centre, shading from dark to light blue. Change to 1 strand white and work 1 row, then change to yellow and work with each shade of yellow towards the centre. Work veins on petals in split stitch using 1 strand of dark blue.

Flower centre

Work centre in French knots with 2 strands of thread (1 strand each of dark yellow and gold together).

DAHLIA DOUBLE

(plate 125 from Choix des plus belles fleurs et des plus beaux fruits)

Materials

- fabric in ecru, 10 x 10 inches (25 x 25 cm)
- DMC stranded cottons in colours listed in key
- needles
    embroidery size 10, for single strand
    embroidery size 9, for 2 strands
    straw size 4, for French knots
- padding

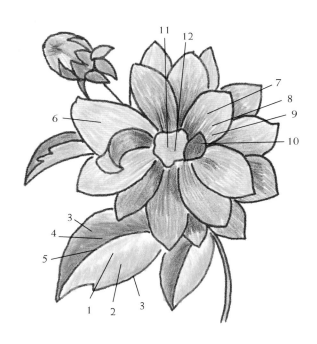

Key	Colour	DMC no		Key	Colour	DMC no
1	Pale green	3348		8	Red	356
2	Light green	989		9	Dark red	3830
3	Green	988		10	Very dark red	3777
4	Dark green	987		11	Light gold	3821
5	Very dark green	319		12	Gold	783
6	Pale red	758				
7	Light red	3778				

■ Padded areas

▨ Padded areas using satin stitch

▱ Directional and detail lines

Note: the colours used in the colour key are not accurately matched to DMC thread colours, and are intended as a shading guide only.

Stems

Work stems in adjoining rows of stem stitch using pale green, green and dark green.

Bud

Outline bud in split stitch using 1 strand of dark red. Fill bud areas in satin stitch using all shades of red.

Bud calyx

Outline sepals in split stitch using 1 strand dark of green. Fill sepals in satin stitch using each shade of green. Work 3 woven picots at spaced intervals in 1 strand of light and dark green together.

Leaves

Outline leaves in split stitch using 1 strand of dark green. Pad leaves as shown. Fill leaves in long and short stitch using 1 strand of each shade of green. Work centre veins in split stitch using 1 strand of very dark green.

Petals

Outline petals in split stitch using 1 strand of dark red. Pad petals as shown. Fill petals in long and short stitch using 1 strand of each shade of red. Work shadows on one side of petals in split stitch, using 1 strand of very dark red and referring to the photo for extra guidance.

Centre

Work centre in French knots using 2 strands (light gold and gold) together.

(plate 40 from Choix des plus belles fleurs et des plus beaux fruits)

Materials

- fabric in ecru, 10 x 10 inches (25 x 25 cm)
- DMC stranded cottons in colours listed in key
- needles
    embroidery size 10, for single strand
    embroidery size 9, for 2 strands
    straw size 4, for French knots
- padding

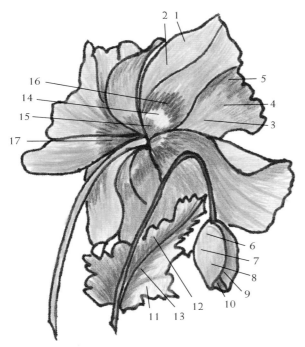

Key	Colour	DMC no
1	Pale red	352
2	Light red	351
3	Red	350
4	Dark red	349
5	Very dark red	817
6	Pale green	3817
7	Light green	907
8	Green	906
9	Dark green	905

Key	Colour	DMC no
10	Very dark green	904
11	Light blue-green	564
12	Blue-green	563
13	Dark blue-green	562
14	Light blue	3753
15	Blue	932
16	Dark blue	931
17	Very dark blue	930

■ *Padded areas*

▨ *Padded areas using satin stitch*

◹ *Directional and detail lines*

Note: the colours used in the colour key are not accurately matched to DMC thread colours, and are intended as a shading guide only.

Petals

Outline petals in split stitch using 1 strand red. Pad petals as shown. Fill petals in long and short stitch using 1 strand of each shade of red.

Petal centre

Work blue/green petal centres over the red in long and short stitch in 1 strand of each shade of blue. Work a few pale green lines against the stem.

Blue-green leaf

Outline leaf in split stitch using 1 strand of dark blue-green. Pad leaf as shown. Fill leaf in long and short stitch using 1 strand of each shade of blue-green. Work centre vein in split stitch using 1 strand of dark blue-green.

Stems

Work stems in adjoining rows of stem stitch using 1 strand of each shade of green.

Bud

Outline bud in split stitch using 1 strand of very dark green. Double pad bud (cut two pieces of padding, 1 smaller than the other, with smaller piece positioned beneath larger piece). Fill bud with long and short stitch using 1 strand of each shade of green.

(plate 35 from Choix des plus belles fleurs et des plus beaux fruits)

Materials

- fabric in ecru, 12 x 12 inches (30 x 30 cm)
- DMC stranded cottons in colours listed in key
- needles
  embroidery size 10, for single strand
  embroidery size 9, for 2 strands
  straw size 4, for French knots
- padding

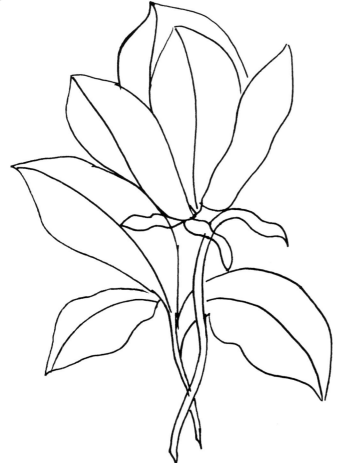

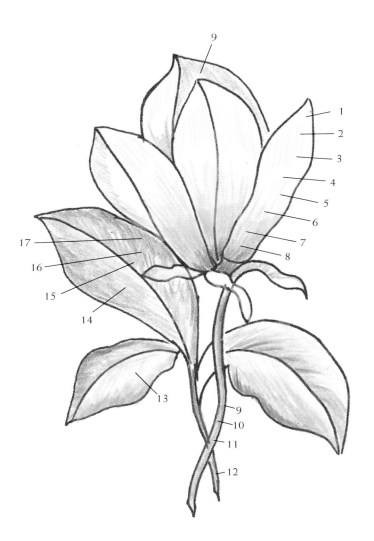

Key	Colour	DMCno
1	Off white	3865
2	Ecru	3866
3	Dark ecru	3033
4	Very dark ecru	3782
5	Pale pink	819
6	Light pink	3713
7	Pink	761
8	Dark pink	760
9	Pale brown	3864
10	Brown	3863
11	Dark brown	3862
12	Pink-brown	3064
13	Pale green	5224
14	Light green	522
15	Green	3364
16	Dark green	3362
17	Very dark green	520

Note: the colours used in the colour key are not accurately matched to DMC thread colours, and are intended as a shading guide only.

Stems

Work stems in adjoining rows of stem stitch using 1 strand of each shade of brown, and shading from dark to light.

Leaves

Outline leaves in split stitch in 1 strand of dark green. Fill leaves in long and short stitch using 1 strand of each shade of green. Work centre vein in split stitch in 1 strand of light green. Work the two small leaves at base of flower in satin stitch in 1 strand of green following the photograph.

Petals

Outline petals in 2 strands of off white. Pad petals as shown. Work back petals first, working forward. Fill large petals in long and short stitch, using 1 strand of each shade from off white through ecru and beige to the pinks. Shade from light to dark. Work small petals at base in satin stitch in 1 strand of pink for left

petal, pale pink for centre petal and ecru for the one on the right. Work centre veins of left and central petals in split stitch, using 1 strand of dark beige.

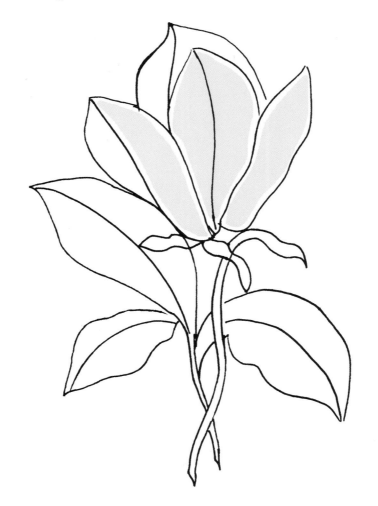

■	*Padded areas*
▨	*Padded areas using satin stitch*
╱	*Directional and detail lines*

(from Les Liliacées)

Materials

- fabric in ecru, 12 x 12 inches (30 x 30 cm)
- DMC stranded cottons in colours listed in key
- needles
    embroidery size 10, for single strand
    embroidery size 9, for 2 strands
    straw size 4, for French knots
- padding

	Padded areas
▨	Padded areas using satin stitch
▨	Directional and detail lines

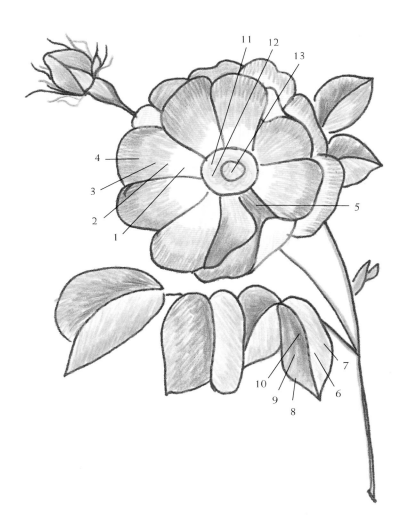

Key	Colour	DMC no
1	Light pink	3354
2	Pink	3733
3	Dark pink	3687
4	Very dark pink	3803
5	Maroon	902
6	Pale green	3348
7	Light green	471
8	Green	470
9	Dark green	469
10	Very dark green	936
11	Yellow	725
12	Gold	783
13	Dark gold	780

Note: the colours used in the colour key are not accurately matched to DMC thread colours, and are intended as a shading guide only.

Stems

Work stems in adjoining rows of stem stitch using 1 strand of each shade of green, and shading from dark to light. Use 1 strand of pink to work the thorns, from the centre of the stem outward in one small stitch.

Leaves

Outline leaves in split stitch using 2 strands of light green. Pad leaves as shown. Work back leaves first, working forward. Fill leaves in long and short stitch using 1 strand of each shade of green. Work centre veins in split stitch in 1 strand of light green.

Petals

Outline petals in split stitch using 2 strands pink. Pad petals as shown. Work back petals first, working forward. Fill petals with long and short stitch in each shade from light pink to maroon, shading from light to dark towards outer edges. Work smaller petal areas in satin stitch. Outline front petals in split stitch in 1 strand of light pink to highlight. Shade centres by working long stitches with 1 strand dark pink over the first layer of stitching.

Rosebud

Outline bud in split stitch in 1 strand of light pink. Fill bud with long and short stitch, using each shade of pink. Outline calyx and sepals in split stitch with 1 strand of dark green. Work the fine sepal tips in adjoining rows of stem stitch in green. Fill sepals and calyx in long and short stitch in 1 strand of shades of green.

Flower centre

Using 1 strand each of yellow and dark gold together in needle, work long straight stitches from central point to outer edge of outer circle. Fill small central area with French knots in 2 strands of gold. Work outer circle in French knots using 2 strands of each shade of gold and yellow.

IRIS PALE

(plate 29 from Choix des plus belles fleurs et des plus beaux fruits)

Materials

- fabric in ecru, 12 x 12 inches (30 x 30 cm)
- DMC stranded cottons in colours listed in key
- needles

    embroidery size 10, for single strand
    embroidery size 9, for 2 strands
    straw size 4, for French knots

- padding

IRIS PALE • tracing outline • padding guide

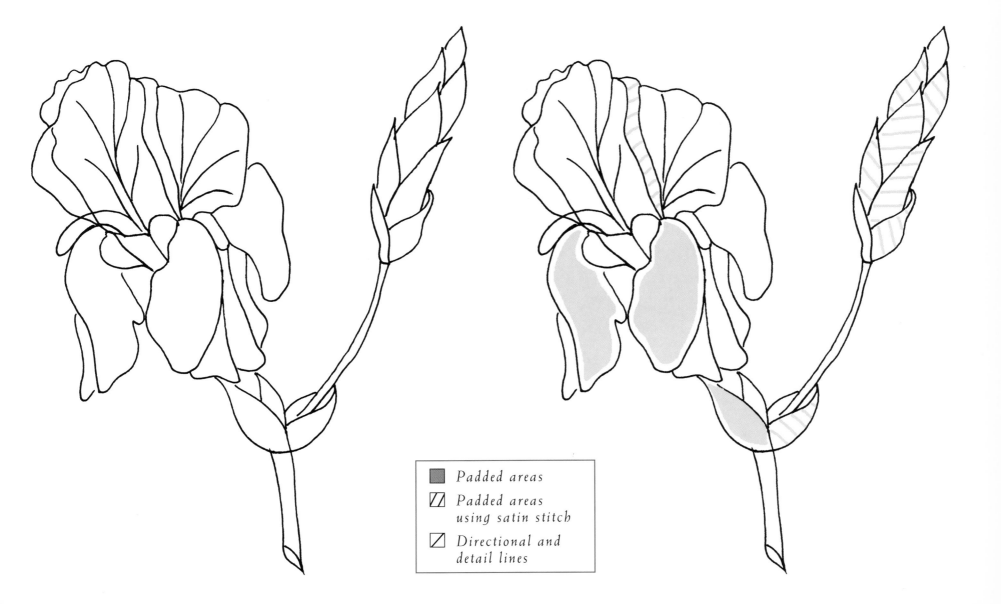

Padded areas

⧄ Padded areas
using satin stitch

⧄ Directional and
detail lines

Key	Colour	DMC no
1	Pale blue	3747
2	Light blue	341
3	Blue	3839
4	Dark blue	3838
5	Very dark blue	792
6	Light yellow	744
7	Yellow	3821
8	Dark yellow	783
9	Very dark yellow	781
10	Pale green	772
11	Light green	989
12	Green	3346
13	Dark green	3345
14	Light beige	677
15	Beige	3046
16	Dark beige	3045

Note: the colours used in the colour key are not accurately matched to DMC thread colours, and are intended as a shading guide only.

Stems

Work stems in adjoining rows of stem stitch using 1 strand of each shade of green.

Bud

Outline bud in split stitch in 1 strand of dark blue. Pad as shown. Fill bud petals in long and short stitch in shades of blue. Outline sepals surrounding bud in split stitch in 1 strand of dark green. Fill with long and short stitch in shades of green.

Bracts

Outline the papery bracts surrounding the bud sepals and stem joint in 1 strand of dark beige. Pad as shown. Work bracts in long and short stitch using 1 strand of each shade of beige.

Flower petals

Outline petals in split stitch in 1 strand of light blue. Pad petals as shown. Fill petals in long and short stitch, using all the shades of blue. Work the left side of each petal first, shading from light to dark towards the centre vein. Work the right sides, working from light to dark towards the outer edges. Work the centre vein in adjoining rows of split stitch, each in 1 strand of pale green and light green. Work outer edges of small petals in satin stitch in 1 strand of blue.

Stamens

Fill stamens with French knots in 2 strands of each shade of yellow, shading from light to dark.

AMARYLLIS BRÉSILIENNE

(plate 14 from Choix des plus belles fleurs et des plus beaux fruits)

Materials

- fabric in ecru, 12 x 12 inches (30 x 30 cm)
- DMC stranded cottons in colours listed in key
- needles
    embroidery size 10, for single strand
    embroidery size 9, for 2 strands
    straw size 4, for bullion knots
- padding

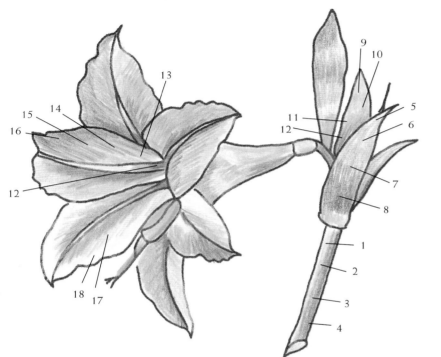

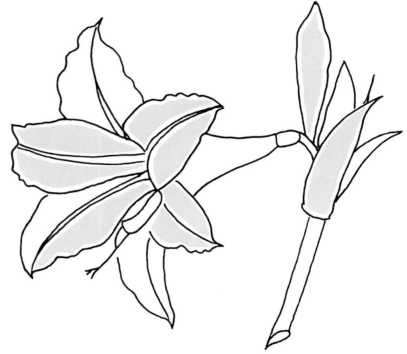

Key	Colour	DMCno	Key	Colour	DMCno
1	Pale grey-green	928	10	Green	3347
2	Light grey-green	927	11	Dark green	3345
3	Grey-green	926	12	Light gold-green	734
4	Dark grey-green	3768	13	Pale red	352
5	Pale lilac	3743	14	Light red	3712
6	Light lilac	3042	15	Red	3328
7	Lilac	3861	16	Dark red	347
8	Dark lilac	3860	17	Peach	353
9	Light green	3348	18	Light peach	3770

◼ *Padded areas*

▨ *Padded areas using satin stitch*

▧ *Directional and detail lines*

Note: the colours used in the colour key are not accurately matched to DMC thread colours, and are intended as a shading guide only.

Stem

Work main stem in adjoining rows of stem stitch in 1 strand of each shade of grey-green. Work short stem at base of open flower in adjoining rows of stem stitch in 1 strand of lilac.

Buds

Outline the two green buds in split stitch in 1 strand of dark green. Fill buds in long and short stitch in shades of green. Outline the three lilac buds in split stitch in 1 strand of dark lilac. Pad buds as shown. Fill these buds in long and short stitch in shades of lilac.

Centre veins

Work veins in adjacent rows of stem stitch in light peach, peach and light gold-green.

Base of flower

Outline sections in split stitch using 1 strand of green. Fill small section in satin stitch, large section in long and short stitch, in shades of green, shading into red at base of flower.

Petals

Outline petals in split stitch using 1 strand of dark red. Pad petals as shown. Working from centre vein towards outer edge of petal, fill petals with long and short stitch using all the shades from pale red through to light peach. Work the centre veins in adjoining rows of stem stitch in 1 strand of light peach, peach and greens, following the colour chart.

Flower centre

Work centre in bullion knots, using 1 strand each of peach and red together. Using 2 strands of light gold-green, work random stitches in seeding stitch and 1 long stitch as shown for stamens.

(plate 47 from Choix des plus belles fleurs et des plus beaux fruits)

Materials

fabric in ecru, 12 x 12 inches (30 x 30 cm)

DMC stranded cottons in colours listed in key

needles

    embroidery size 10, for single strand

    embroidery size 9, for 2 strands

    straw size 4, for French knots

padding

Key	Colour	DMCno	Key	Colour	DMCno
1	Pale brown	842	8	Very dark green	936
2	Light brown	841	9	Light yellow	3822
3	Dark brown	3781	10	Yellow	3821
4	Pale green	472	11	Dark yellow	3820
5	Light green	471	12	Very dark yellow	3852
6	Green	470	13	Rust	781
7	Dark green	469	14	Dark brown machine embroidery thread	

■ *Padded areas*

▨ *Padded areas using satin stitch*

▧ *Directional and detail lines*

Note: the colours used in the colour key are not accurately matched to DMC thread colours, and are intended as a shading guide only.

Stems

Work stems in adjoining rows of stem stitch using 1 strand of each shade of brown.

Leaves

Outline leaves and sepals in split stitch using 1 strand of dark green. Pad areas as shown. Fill leaves in long and short stitch using 1 strand of each shade of green, and shading from light to dark towards centre veins. Work centre veins in split stitch using 1 strand of dark green. Outline highlights of smaller leaves (sepals) in split stitch in 1 strand of pale green. Work 3 picots below profile flower to add depth (picots are not shown on working diagrams—see photo), using 1 strand each of light green and dark green together.

Flowers

Outline petals in split stitch using 1 strand of dark yellow. Pad petals as shown. Fill petals in long and short stitch, using 1 strand of each shade of yellow, and rust. Work from outer edges towards centre. Outline some petals in split stitch, as shown in the photograph, using 1 strand of light yellow.

Flower centre

Work centre in seeding stitch in 2 strands of thread, in shades of yellow, green and rust. Take 1 strand of dark brown machine embroidery thread and work single French knots, scattered to give depth.

(from Les Liliacées)

Materials

- fabric in ecru, 12 x 12 inches (30 x 30 cm)
- DMC stranded cottons in colours listed in key
- needles
    embroidery size 10, for single strand
    embroidery size 9, for 2 strands
    straw size 4, for French knots
- padding

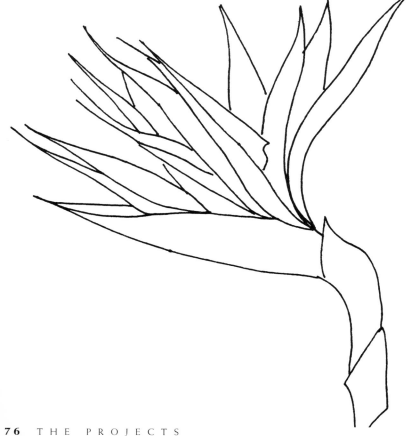

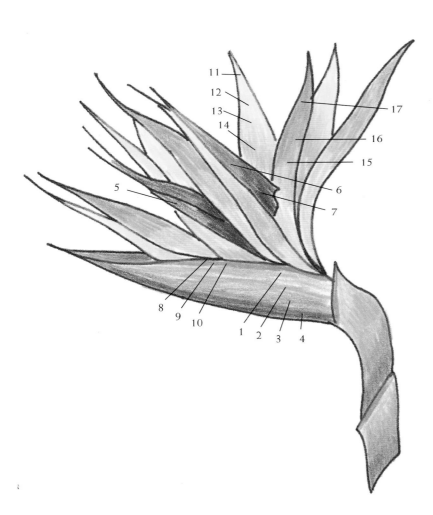

Key	Colour	DMCno
1	Light green	772
2	Green	3364
3	Dark green	3363
4	Very dark green	3362
5	Light blue	3755
6	Blue	322
7	Dark blue	311
8	Light rust	3778
9	Rust	356
10	Dark rust	355
11	Light yellow	744
12	Yellow	743
13	Dark yellow	742
14	Light orange	741
15	Orange	721
16	Dark orange	720
17	Very dark orange	920

Note: the colours used in the colour key are not accurately matched to DMC thread colours, and are intended as a shading guide only.

Petals

Outline petals in split stitch using 1 strand of dark orange. Fill yellow and orange petals in long and short stitch using 1 strand of each shade of yellow and orange. Work back petals first, working forward. Shade from light to dark. Work blue petals in shades of blue.

Flower bract, stem and leaf

Outline the three areas in split stitch using 1 strand of dark green. Pad as shown. Fill each section in long and short stitch, using 1 strand of each shade of green. Work upper edges in adjoining rows of split stitch, using 1 strand of each shade of rust.

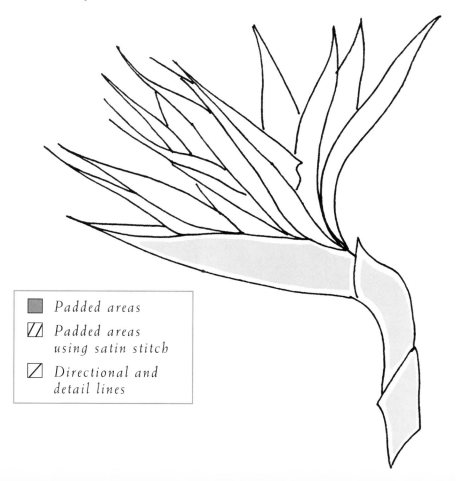

■	Padded areas
▨	Padded areas using satin stitch
◹	Directional and detail lines

VARIÉTÉS DE ROSE JAUNE

(plate 92 from Choix des plus belles fleurs et des plus beaux fruits)

Materials

- fabric in ecru, 12 x 12 inches (30 x 30 cm)
- DMC stranded cottons in colours listed in key
- needles
    embroidery size 10, for single strand
    embroidery size 9, for 2 strands
    straw size 4, for French knots
- padding

Padded areas

Padded areas
using satin stitch

Directional and
detail lines

Key	Colour	DMC no
1	Cream	746
2	Pale yellow	3027
3	Light yellow	727
4	Yellow	3822
5	Dark yellow	3820
6	Pale pink	3770
7	Light pink	754
8	Pink	758
9	Dark pink	3778
10	Very dark pink	3830
11	Light green	369
12	Green	368
13	Dark green	367
14	Very dark green	319

Note: the colours used in the colour key are not accurately matched to DMC thread colours, and are intended as a shading guide only.

Stems

Work pink stems in adjoining rows of stem stitch in 1 strand each of the medium to dark pinks. Work green stems in adjoining rows of stem stitch in 1 strand of each shade of green. Work thorns in small straight stitches in pink and dark pink. Refer to the colour photo for the placement of the thorns.

Buds

Outline the two pink buds in split stitch in 1 strand of pink. Fill bud petals in long and short stitch or satin stitch, as appropriate for the size of the area, in 1 strand of shades of pink. Outline the yellow bud in split stitch in 1 strand of yellow. Fill petals in long and short stitch or satin stitch, as appropriate, in 1 strand of shades of yellow.

Leaves and sepals

Outline leaves and sepals in split stitch in 1 strand of green. Pad leaves as shown. Work fine areas at tips of sepals in split stitch in 1 strand of dark green, and fill the rest of the sepal areas with long and short stitch in shades of green. Follow diagram carefully for the pink areas on some leaves. Work leaves in long and short stitch in 1 strand of each shade of green, filling tips of some leaves in pink. Work areas of pink where shown.

Pink rose

Outline petals in pink. Fill larger petals in long and short stitch using 1 strand of each shade of pink. Use satin stitch in the smaller areas.

Yellow rose

Outline petals in split stitch in 1 strand of yellow. Pad petals as shown. Fill petals in long and short stitch in 1 strand of each shade of yellow.

(plate 109 from Choix des plus belles fleurs et des plus beaux fruits)

Materials

fabric in ecru, 12 x 12 inches (30 x 30 cm)
DMC stranded cottons in colours listed in key
needles
    embroidery size 10, for single strand
    embroidery size 9, for 2 strands
    straw size 4, for French knots

padding

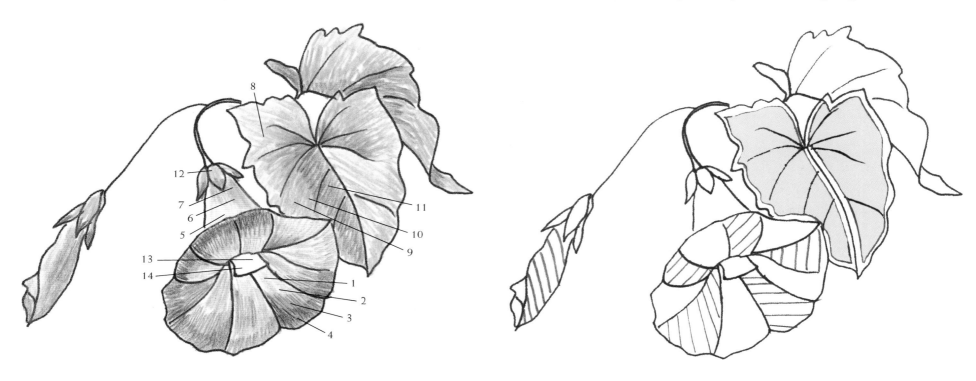

Key	Colour	DMC no	Key	Colour	DMC no
1	Pale lilac	3743	8	Light green	772
2	Lilac	3042	9	Green	3348
3	Dark lilac	3041	10	Dark green	3347
4	Very dark lilac	3740	11	Very dark green	3345
5	Light pink	3727	12	Green-gold	733
6	Pink	316	13	Pale yellow	3078
7	Dark pink	3726	14	Yellow	727

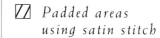 Padded areas

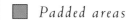 Padded areas using satin stitch

Directional and detail lines

Note: the colours used in the colour key are not accurately matched to DMC thread colours, and are intended as a shading guide only.

Stems

Work stems in adjoining rows of stem stitch in 1 strand of green-gold and medium green. Leave the tendril until the leaves have been embroidered.

Leaves and calyces

Outline leaves, and the calyces of flower and bud, in split stitch in 1 strand of dark green. Fill calyces and leaves in long and short stitch in 1 strand of each shade of green. Work centre veins in split stitch in 1 strand of light green.

Tendril

Work tendril in 2 adjoining rows of stem stitch in 1 strand of green.

Bud

Outline bud in dark lilac. Pad bud as shown. Fill bud in long and short stitch in shades of lilac.

Flower

Outline all sections in split stitch in 1 strand of medium lilac. Pad areas as shown. Fill sections in long and short stitch in each shade of lilac. Work over some sections as shown in shades of pink.

Flower centre

Work centre in long straight stitches in 1 strand of pale yellow. Work French knots in 2 strands of yellow in throat of flower.

ANEMONE SIMPLE

(plate 37 from Choix des plus belles fleurs et des plus beaux fruits)

Materials

- fabric in ecru, 14 x 14 inches (35 x 35 cm)
- DMC stranded cottons in colours listed in key
- needles
    embroidery size 10, for single strand
    embroidery size 9, for 2 strands
    straw size 4, for French knots
- padding

ANEMONE SIMPLE • padding guide

■	Padded areas
▨	Padded areas using satin stitch
◹	Directional and detail lines

ANEMONE SIMPLE • thread & colour key

Key	Colour	DMC no
1	Light blue	793
2	Blue	792
3	Dark blue	791
4	Very dark blue	823
5	Pale red	3705
6	Light red	666
7	Red	321
8	Dark red	498
9	White	blanc
10	Pale pink	819
11	Light pink	3713
12	Pink	761
13	Dark pink	760
14	Pale yellow	745
15	Yellow	744
16	Pale lilac	3747
17	Light lilac	341
18	Mauve	3042
19	Light grey-green	524
20	Grey-green	522
21	Dark grey-green	520
22	Light green	3348
23	Green	3347
24	Dark green	3346
25	Very dark green	3345

Note: the colours used in the colour key are not accurately matched to DMC thread colours, and are intended as a shading guide only.

Stems

Work stems in adjoining rows of stem stitch, using 1 strand of each shade of grey-green for the stems on the right, and 1 strand of each shade of green for the stems on the left and at the front.

Leaves

Outline leaves in split stitch using 1 strand of dark green. Fill leaves in long and short stitch with 1 strand using each shade of green. Shade from centre towards outer edge of leaf.

Dark blue flower

Outline petals in split stitch using 1 strand of light blue. Pad petals as shown. Fill petals in long and short stitch using 1 strand of each shade of blue. Outline some petals in split stitch with 1 strand of light blue.

Red flower

Outline petals in split stitch using 1 strand of red. Pad petals as shown. Fill petals in long and short stitch using 1 strand of each shade of red. Outline some petals in split stitch in 1 strand of light red. Fill centre of flower with French knots, using 2 strands of blue and dark blue.

Pink and white flower

Outline petals in split stitch using 1 strand of pale pink. Pad petals as shown. Fill petals in long and short stitch using 1 strand of each shade from white through pink to yellow. Outline some petals in split stitch using 1 strand of white.

White and blue flowers

Outline all petals in split stitch using 1 strand of light blue. Pad petals as shown. Fill petals in long and short stitch using 1 strand of white and each shade of blue. Shade over some areas in pink and mauve. Outline some petals in split stitch in 1 strand of white. Fill flower centres in French knots, using 2 strands of blue, 2 strands of medium blue, and 1 strand of pale blue together with 1 strand of dark blue.

LE LYS BLANC

(plate 7 from Choix des plus belles fleurs et des plus beaux fruits)

Materials

- fabric in ecru, 14 x 14 inches (35 x 35 cm)
- DMC stranded cottons in colours listed in key
- needles
    embroidery size 10, for single strand
    embroidery size 9, for 2 strands
    straw size 4, for bullion knots
- padding

▨	*Padded areas*
◪	*Padded areas using satin stitch*
◿	*Directional and detail lines*

Key	Colour	DMC no
1	White	blanc
2	Off white	3865
3	Ecru	3866
4	Beige	3024
5	Dark beige	3023
6	Pale brown	647
7	Light green	3348
8	Green	989
9	Light lime green	472
10	Lime green	471
11	Light yellow	744
12	Yellow	743
13	Dark yellow	783
14	Pale seafoam	504
15	Light seafoam	503
16	Seafoam	502
17	Dark seafoam	501
18	Very dark seafoam	500
19	Orange	922

Note: the colours used in the colour key are not accurately matched to DMC thread colours, and are intended as a shading guide only.

Stems

Work stems in adjoining rows of stem stitch using 1 strand of each shade of seafoam (a range of blue-green colours).

Buds

Outline buds in 1 strand of light green. Pad buds as shown. Fill buds in long and short stitch using 1 strand in each shade of white, light yellow and the greens. Define ridges on buds with long straight stitches in pale brown as indicated on diagram.

Leaves

Outline leaves in split stitch using 1 strand dark seafoam. Pad the lowest leaf only. Fill leaves in long and short stitch using 1 strand in all the shades of seafoam. Work centre veins in split stitch in 1 strand of dark green.

Flowers

Outline petals in split stitch using 1 strand of beige. Pad areas as shown. Fill petals in long and short stitch using 1 strand of each shade from white through to pale brown. Work centre veins in split stitch in 1 strand of pale brown. Work pale green over the outer petal bases of the two upper flowers, and within the throat of the bottom flower.

Flower centres

Work flower centres in bullion stitch using 2 strands of all shades of yellow and orange. Work straight stitches for stamens in yellow and small seeding stitches at the tips of the stamens in orange. Work an additional bullion stitch using 1 strand of light lime green and 1 strand of lime green together. This bullion should come from the centre of the orange bullions as shown in the photo. Work one seed stitch in lime green at the top of the bullion.